D1607171

Life Skills

Volunteering

Giving Back

by Robert Wandberg, PhD

Consultants:
Roberta Brack Kaufman, EdD
Dean, College of Education
Concordia University
St. Paul, Minnesota

Millie Shepich, MPH, CHES
Health Educator and District Health Coordinator
Waubonsie Valley High School
Aurora, Illinois

LifeMatters
an imprint of Capstone Press
Mankato, Minnesota

Thank you to the students of the Hennepin County Home School, who provided valuable feedback for the direction this book has taken.

LifeMatters Books are published by Capstone Press
PO Box 669 • 151 Good Counsel Drive • Mankato, Minnesota 56002
http://www.capstone-press.com

Printed in the United States of America

Library of Congress Cataloging-in-Publication Data
Wandberg, Robert.
     Volunteering: giving back / by Robert Wandberg.
          p.   cm. — (Life skills)
     Includes bibliographical references and index.
     ISBN 0-7368-1022-6
     1. Teenage volunteers in social service—Juvenile literature. 2. Volunteer workers in social service—Juvenile literature. 3. Volunteers—Juvenile literature. 4. Voluntarism—Juvenile literature. [1. Voluntarism.] I. Title. II. Series.
     HV40.42 .W36 2002
     361.3′7—dc21   00-012917
                                            CIP

Summary: Shows many ways teens can volunteer in order to give of themselves. Includes information on volunteering as well as different areas of volunteerism, such as hospitals, hot lines, environment, and blood or organ donation. Describes practical tips to get started.

Staff Credits
Charles Pederson, editor; Adam Lazar, designer; Kim Danger, photo researcher

Photo Credits
Cover: ©Tim Yoon
NovaStock/Photo Agora, 49
Photri Inc, 26, 34, 54/©Tom McCarthy, 13; ©Fotopic, 31; ©Skjold, 59
Pictor, 53/©Bob Daemmrich, 18; ©Paul Conklin, 52; ©Bob Daemmrich Photo., Inc., 56
Unicorn Stock Photos/©Jeff Greenberg, 6; ©Charles E. Schmidt, 11; ©Steve Bourgeois, 29;
©Jim Riddle, 35; ©Chris Boylan, 42
©Tim Yoon, 5, 15, 21, 33, 41, 51

A 0 9 8 7 6 5 4 3 2 1

Table of Contents

1 | Getting Started | 4

2 | The Next Step | 14

3 | Volunteering: It's About People | 20

4 | Volunteering for the Community and Environment | 32

5 | Volunteering by Donation | 40

6 | Practical Volunteering | 50

For More Information | 60

Glossary | 62

Index | 63

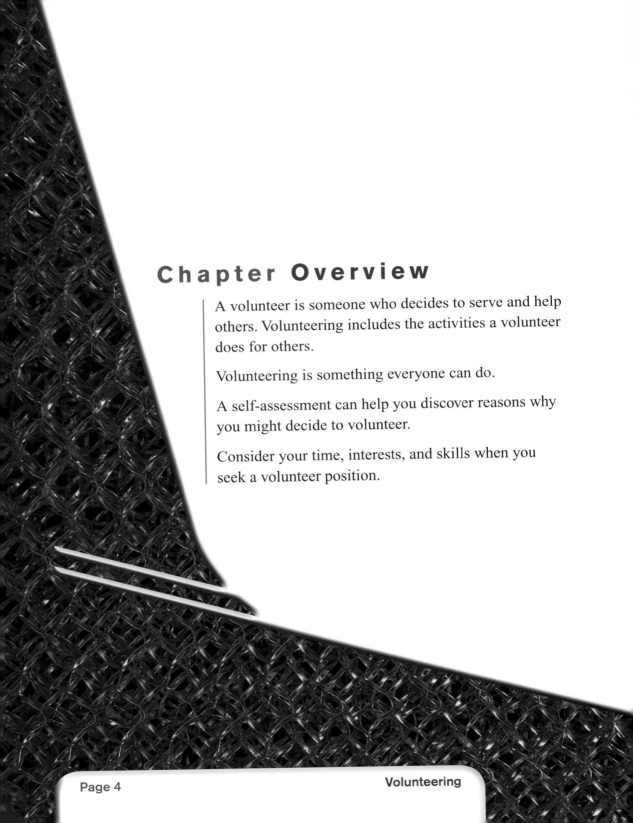

Chapter Overview

A volunteer is someone who decides to serve and help others. Volunteering includes the activities a volunteer does for others.

Volunteering is something everyone can do.

A self-assessment can help you discover reasons why you might decide to volunteer.

Consider your time, interests, and skills when you seek a volunteer position.

CHAPTER 1

☼

Getting Started

Teens volunteer for many reasons. They may want to help others who can't do something themselves. A medical or environmental issue may get teens involved. Teens who volunteer can make a difference for the world and other people. In this chapter, you'll learn how to get started in volunteering. Such **StartingMatters** include identifying your interests, the possibilities, and the limits.

Volunteers may do many things, such as collect and pack food for the homeless.

"I volunteer at a clinic that helps families who can't afford shots or don't have insurance. I greet people, answer phones, and explain the services our clinic offers. I love to see people's faces when I've helped them. Volunteering gives me an awesome feeling inside."

What's It About?

A volunteer is someone who performs a service of his or her own free will. Volunteering is the activities that a volunteer does for other people. Cleaning a park, painting someone's house, collecting food, and raising money for the homeless are examples of volunteering.

Volunteering helps others, but it also may help the volunteer. Maybe you're active in your neighborhood crime watch. Then, your home is protected while you protect your neighbors' homes. Adding your effort to that of other people can have a big effect.

Some people think that volunteering is only for retired people. Some people think it's only for rich people, sports heroes, or celebrities. Nothing is further from the truth. People from all walks of life volunteer. Look at these examples.

A homeless man raised $1,000 to repay a homeless shelter that took him in.

An 8-year-old collected 12 truckloads of toys for flood victims.

A 16-year-old helped organize a blood drive at his school.

Teens are some of the most wanted and effective volunteers. You might think volunteering isn't for you. Don't think of it only as doing something for people who are less fortunate than you. Think of it as an exchange. Most people need help at some point in their life. Today, you may be the person who can help. Tomorrow, you may need someone's help. You also can get benefits yourself from volunteering. For example, you may be able to learn new skills or gain new friends.

Self-Assessments and Volunteering

To help you determine why you might volunteer, try this quick self-assessment. Self-assessments are tests that can help people know themselves better. Self-assessments cover many different topics. Some are based on medical information. Some are about knowledge, attitudes, or behavior.

Taking occasional self-assessments can help you see if you need or want to change anything. The key is that you're the only one who decides what the information means. The following self-assessment can help you see possible reasons for volunteering.

Why Do I Volunteer?

Read items 1–21 below. On a separate piece of paper, write the best answer for each item as it applies to you.

I would volunteer:

1. To feel needed	Yes	Maybe	No
2. To share knowledge or skill	Yes	Maybe	No
3. To show commitment to a cause	Yes	Maybe	No
4. To improve leadership skills	Yes	Maybe	No
5. Because of pressure from friends or relatives	Yes	Maybe	No
6. To keep myself busy	Yes	Maybe	No
7. For personal recognition	Yes	Maybe	No
8. Because no one else can do it	Yes	Maybe	No
9. To learn something new	Yes	Maybe	No
10. To help a stranger	Yes	Maybe	No

Volunteering

There are several national service days in the United States. Make a Difference Day falls on the last Saturday in October. On this day, volunteer activities occur all over the world. It has been the United States' largest day of volunteering and community service.

Youth Service Day occurs on the third weekend of April. It honors young volunteers and invites people to do their part. The For More Information section, starting on page 60, has other volunteering resources you can check out.

11. To help a friend or relative	Yes	Maybe	No
12. For personal growth and self-esteem	Yes	Maybe	No
13. To make new friends	Yes	Maybe	No
14. To explore a career	Yes	Maybe	No
15. For fun	Yes	Maybe	No
16. For religious reasons	Yes	Maybe	No
17. To earn school credit	Yes	Maybe	No
18. To do what I love	Yes	Maybe	No
19. To feel good	Yes	Maybe	No
20. To be part of a school or community team	Yes	Maybe	No
21. Because there's a need in the community	Yes	Maybe	No

Look at your answers. The ones you answered with "yes" may give you a clue about the kinds of volunteer service most important to you.

AT A GLANCE

Several activities associated with volunteering can strengthen the fitness of your body, heart, or lungs. For example, you might walk while delivering brochures in your neighborhood. If you want to know how many calories per hour your volunteer work uses, look at the chart below.

The number after each item shows about how many calories that a 150-pound (68-kilogram) person uses per hour.

Calories Used per Hour for Some Activities

Biking (6 miles or 9.6 kilometers per hour)	240
Dancing	160
Running (5 miles or 8 kilometers per hour)	740
Walking (3 miles or 4.8 kilometers per hour)	320

Other Considerations

There are some other things to think about before you volunteer. These include how much time you have, your interests, and your skills.

Time

Decide how much time you have and when you're available. Can you volunteer only after school? on weekends? during school breaks? during the summer?

Some volunteer assignments require lots of time. You can do others in a short time, even a day. If it's your first volunteer job, begin with a shorter time commitment. Many organizations have work that volunteers can do evenings, weekends, or for short periods. Be honest with yourself and your organization. Don't volunteer if you don't have the time.

One important thing to consider before you volunteer is how much time you have.

Interests

The best volunteer experience involves things you enjoy. If you enjoy it, volunteering will be more fulfilling. You'll probably stick with it longer.

It's equally important to know what you don't want. For example, if you dislike animals, don't volunteer with an animal humane society. And you don't have to say yes just because someone offers you a job. The happier you are about what you're doing, the better worker you'll be.

Rudo, Age 13

Rudo wanted to volunteer but wasn't sure what he wanted to do. His uncle asked him some questions. "What are you interested in? Is there any place around here that can use that talent? Could you start your own group?" Rudo was glad he asked his uncle. Those questions helped him get his thinking straight.

Skills

Do you want to volunteer for something that uses your skills? Almost every skill is needed somewhere. Or do you want to do something completely new? If so, you might not want to volunteer for work that uses the same skills you use every day.

Some volunteer positions require your knowledge of a task, such as working with a computer. However, many positions need great people skills, too. For example, are you nonjudgmental, good at listening, cheery, or supportive?

As a volunteer, you can experiment with new activities. Do you wish you could learn something new? Some organizations will gladly assign you to something as a beginner. They know that you'll be enthusiastic about tackling something new. This is one way that volunteering develops skills and is fun. By testing yourself in different ways, you can get a fresh perspective on the everyday world.

Even if you don't have specific work skills, you still can volunteer. Organizations always need volunteers with good people skills.

Do you agree that volunteering is an exchange? Explain.

What are your most important reasons for volunteering? Why?

Do you think time, interest, or skills is the most important consideration in volunteering for a job? Why?

Chapter Overview

Many different areas need volunteers. After discovering your reasons to volunteer, the next step is to check out different volunteer areas.

When you find some interesting organizations, contact them. Speak clearly if you get an answering machine.

You probably will have some questions about the organization. Be sure to ask them. Also, you might need to fill out an application.

Volunteering together is a great way to spend time with friends and family.

Giving

CHAPTER 2

⌖

The Next Step

Do you want to volunteer? That's great. In the last chapter, you looked at yourself and some of the reasons you might have for volunteering. The important thing is that you want to volunteer. The next thing to do is think about areas of interest where you want to volunteer. Let's think of this step as **NextMatters**.

Looking Into Different Areas

Many community organizations and projects could use your help as a volunteer. Look at the areas on the next page and decide if you'd like to explore any of them. If any interest you, check them out at school or in your community. But don't stop there. Remember, the areas—and possibilities—for volunteering are limitless.

Areas of Possible Volunteer Interest

Abused children's organizations	Hospitals
Adoption agencies	Homeless assistance programs
Animal care	Libraries
Physical and emotional disability programs	Neighborhood cleanups
	Nursing homes
Environmental protection	Political organizations
Food and clothing programs	Preschool programs
Gang prevention	Runaway youth assistance
Gardening clubs	Substance abuse prevention and treatment
Group homes	
Holiday toy drives	Teen pregnancy

What's Next?

When you find interesting possibilities, then contact organizations in that area to see if they need volunteer help. Usually, you either call or visit them. If there is a volunteer coordinator, ask to speak with that person.

Calling an organization for information is not the same thing as volunteering. Just calling doesn't mean you have agreed to work with them. If you get a voice message system when you call, leave a message. Here's a sample:

"Hello, my name is [state your name]. I'm a student at [give your school's name]. I heard about your organization from [state how you heard about this organization]. I am interested in learning about volunteer opportunities. Please call me back at [give your telephone number] after [give a time of day when you're home]. Thank you."

Speak slowly and clearly. If you don't hear back in a few days, call again.

What Are the Details?

Decide if you want to visit and see the place before you make a commitment. If you visit, don't be late, and be sure to ask lots of questions. This is the best time to find out the details of the volunteer job. What will you do? When and where will you do it? Who is your supervisor? Does the job fit your schedule and abilities? Could you talk with other volunteers to get their views? Are there any dress requirements? Will you work alone or with others? When would you start? A volunteer coordinator may be able to give you this information. If you don't have time for a long-term commitment, consider volunteering for one-day events.

You'll probably fill out a volunteer application form. You may have to agree not to give away confidential information people share about themselves or the organization. You might need to take a physical exam. You may have to attend a training workshop. If you're under age 18, a parent or guardian may need to sign a permission form.

Be patient if the first job isn't right for you. Different opportunities may exist within the same organization. If nothing still appeals to you, thank the volunteer coordinator for talking with you. Then continue your search somewhere else.

Volunteering with friends is a great way to spend time together.

Volunteering With Family and Friends

You may have many responsibilities to family, school, and friends. With your busy schedule, there may seem to be no time left for volunteering. Try volunteering along with some of your family or friends.

Mari, Age 16

"I got some of my brothers to volunteer with me at the library. Once a week, we take the bus downtown and do whatever the librarians need. We read to little kids, we reshelve books, we show people how to find information. It's one of the few times during the week that we actually get to spend together. I think we've all discovered new talents in ourselves and each other, too. It's helped us think about each other in more positive ways. It's also given us lots of new things to discuss at home."

Choosing a Project With Family or Friends

Don't rush. Take time to consider the volunteer possibilities. Make sure everyone, no matter how young, participates in the discussion.

Is anyone currently volunteering? Is there any interest in expanding that effort to include other friends or family members?

What interests do you share? Explore organizations in your community already working in your interest areas. Consult the telephone directory, the library, teachers, counselors, and neighbors.

Discuss the types of work everyone likes. This is important information when you contact potential volunteer organizations.

Contact several organizations to determine your options, if possible.

Begin with a one-time activity. This is a good test to see how everyone likes volunteering together.

Once you're committed to a volunteer project, take it seriously. Show up when you say you will.

You've taken the next important step. Now you're ready to roll up your sleeves and go to work!

Points to Consider: NextMatters

Do any of the volunteer areas on page 16 appeal to you? Can you think of others?

Describe the process for contacting an organization that interests you.

What questions should you ask before applying for a volunteer job?

Would you find it easier to volunteer alone or with family or friends? Explain.

Chapter Overview

Many people who have a disease need volunteer help.

Organizations that deal with HIV and AIDS often need volunteers.

Millions of people have AIDS worldwide. There are many ways volunteers can help these people.

Volunteering to help the hungry, homeless, or mentally ill can be very rewarding.

CHAPTER 3

☼

Volunteering: It's About People

You may choose to invest your volunteer energy in assisting someone dealing with a disease or other personal crisis. This chapter describes some of these crises, which might be called **PeopleMatters**.

Perhaps you've watched TV or listened to the radio and heard a storm warning. These storms can create danger and hardships for people.

But what about internal storms, which may involve diseases or personal problems? Many of us know people who are having an internal storm. Volunteers can be important for people in a situation like this.

Abe's grandfather was pretty healthy and still able to live in his apartment. However, sometimes he got confused about his medicine, doctors' appointments, and other medical matters. So Abe bought a magnetic card for his grandfather's refrigerator. On it, Abe wrote his grandfather's medicines, when he should take them, and how much. He also wrote the names and telephone numbers of his grandfather's clinic and the nearest hospital. He included names and numbers of friends and relatives his grandfather could call for help.

His grandfather really appreciated the card. He told Abe, "A lot of my friends could use something like this." So Abe made them cards. Abe decided to organize a group from his synagogue. They would make magnets for other older people at home, in hospitals, or in nursing care. He talked to his rabbi, who suggested some ways to do it. After a couple of months, Abe and his group had made medical cards for hundreds of people.

The word *chronic* is from the Greek word *chronos,* which means "time." About 100 million Americans, or about one-third of the U.S. population, have chronic diseases. Chronic diseases such as heart disease and cancer cause the most death and injury in the United States.

People With Diseases Need Help

Many organizations focus on specific diseases or body organs. For example, the American Cancer Society seeks to cure cancer. The Canadian Lung Association provides education on breathing problems. These organizations welcome all volunteers to share information on protecting health.

DID YOU KNOW?

It may be 10 or more years from the time of HIV infection to AIDS. For example, a 16-year-old infected with HIV may not develop AIDS until nearly age 30. It could be much sooner. In the United States, total reported deaths of people with AIDS are 430,441. This includes 425,357 adults and teens and 5,084 children under age 13.

Volunteers may read to patients, play games, help them write letters, or just talk. Some patients may not live long. Volunteers can make the patients' life a little more happy and enjoyable.

Volunteers can teach classes on reducing the risk of infectious and chronic diseases. They may teach cardiopulmonary resuscitation (CPR). This is a technique to revive a person whose heart has stopped beating.

Hospital volunteers may direct visitors to check in, help families in waiting rooms, or provide care for patients.

Volunteers may help with fund-raising events such as walk-a-thons or auctions.

Some teens are interested in a particular disease or condition. Perhaps a relative or friend has multiple sclerosis, birth defects, or Parkinson's disease. Many organizations devote themselves to preventing or controlling such diseases and conditions.

Local telephone directories list health organizations and hospitals. Some of these places conduct volunteer orientations to explain the many available volunteer services and needs.

Epidemics have occurred throughout history. One of the best known of these widespread diseases was the bubonic plague, or the "Black Death." It swept through Europe and parts of Asia in the 14th century. It killed as much as three-quarters of the population in less than 20 years.

A Look at HIV and AIDS

Today, many infectious germs pose new threats to world health. Perhaps you've heard of some of them: Legionnaire's disease, Lyme disease, Ebola. AIDS is another recent epidemic disease.

AIDS is a world and community health issue. As a teen, you may wonder how you can help. There are many ways volunteers can fight the AIDS battle. But first, let's review some basic facts about AIDS.

The human immunodeficiency virus (HIV) causes acquired immune deficiency syndrome (AIDS). This viral infection kills a specific kind of white blood cell called a T-cell. These T-cells fight off a variety of germs. Having fewer T-cells often results in a higher chance of getting life-threatening diseases.

HIV and AIDS are spread through direct contact between people's bodily fluids. These fluids include blood, breast milk, semen, or vaginal fluid. Drug users who share needles also can spread the infection to each other.

How Many People Have AIDS in the United States?

The total of U.S. AIDS cases reported to the Centers for Disease Control and Prevention (CDC) through 1999 is 733,374. Adult and adolescent AIDS cases total 724,656. Of these, 604,843 cases are males and 119,813 cases are females. There were 8,718 AIDS cases reported in children under age 13.

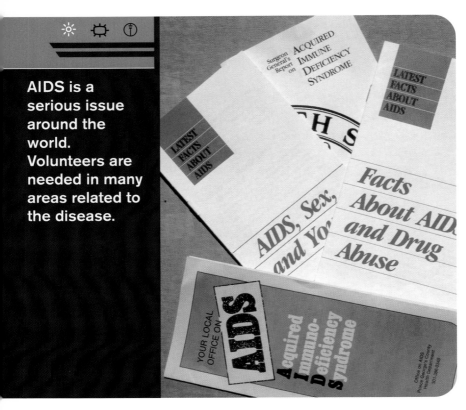

AIDS is a serious issue around the world. Volunteers are needed in many areas related to the disease.

AIDS Around the World

At the end of 1999, the Joint United Nations Programme on HIV/AIDS noted these estimates for HIV:

Since the AIDS epidemic began in the early 1980s, 33.6 million people have gotten HIV/AIDS. This includes 1.2 million children under age 15.

About 16.3 million people have died from AIDS since the epidemic began in the early 1980s. This includes 3.6 million children under age 15.

In 1999, HIV-associated illnesses killed 2.6 million people, including 470,000 children under age 15.

By the end of 1999, there were 11.2 million "AIDS orphans." These are people who before reaching age 15 lose their mother to AIDS. Many of these children also have had their father die of AIDS.

AIDS Cases in the United States by Age, Through June 2000

Under age 5:	6,812
5 to 19:	5,857
20 to 29:	126,105
30 to 39:	337,501
40 to 49:	196,526
50 to 59:	59,089
60 or older:	22,014

Volunteering to Fight AIDS

After understanding the seriousness of this disease, many teens feel the need to join the fight against AIDS. Here are a few ways you could volunteer:

Participate in AIDS walks or bike rides. Friends, family, and others agree to give volunteers a certain amount of money for walking or biking. The money is used for research into ways to control and cure AIDS.

Help with mailings or help answer telephones. You probably would work at the organization's headquarters.

Do household chores for people with AIDS.

Help patients get to medical appointments or do grocery shopping.

Give a talk at school or write in the school newspaper about issues related to AIDS.

Call a local AIDS hot line for other suggestions.

"About 20 teens from my school went to a local shelter for women and children. We wanted to make them feel special, so we offered them manicures, hair braiding, and tea and cookies. We entertained their children with stories, videos, and snacks. It was a fun way to make a difference in someone's life."
—Selena, age 14

Other Internal Storms

Some internal storms people face aren't chronic or infectious diseases. Some involve mental or emotional crises, addictions, hunger, or homelessness.

Providing food to the hungry is a valuable volunteer service. Unfortunately, thousands of people go hungry every day. Many of them are children and the elderly. Experts indicate that the problem isn't a lack of food. It's a lack of volunteers to collect and distribute it. Volunteers also are needed to help with food drives that organizations sponsor. Volunteers can help sort, stock, and pack community food shelves or pantries. Volunteers are needed to serve the food as well.

This is one example of volunteerism that you can do with friends. Most food shelves would welcome you to volunteer a few hours a month. Your volunteer time can be flexible. You can work just once or only a few times a month. Your local food shelf may have a person who specifically coordinates volunteer services.

One way volunteers can work in shelters is by helping take care of children.

Helping the Homeless

Many children, teens, young parents, and adults have no home. Maybe you know someone who is homeless. Maybe you're homeless. Many teens account for the invisible homeless. They live with friends or relatives. They even may sleep in cars or other shelters.

Homeless people often look to the community for help. Community programs and volunteers are needed to provide basic services for the homeless. Often the amount of service a community can provide is directly related to the number of volunteers. The more volunteers there are, the more people who can receive services.

Volunteers are needed in shelters. They can help with child care for homeless children. Volunteers could serve food, help with laundry, or talk with people. They might help the homeless find other services including employment, education, counseling, or medical care. Volunteers are needed to repair, paint, and maintain shelters.

Young homeless people sometimes need tutoring. About one-third of all homeless kids don't attend school regularly. Drop-in centers, temporary housing facilities, or large shelters may offer tutoring programs for kids. Runaway shelters provide a safe place for kids with family problems. Volunteers help by staffing the reception area, answering the telephone, and keeping the shelter working smoothly.

Helping the Mentally Ill

People from young children to the elderly can be sad or depressed and have to deal with problems. Sometimes, people have intense feelings of sadness, hopelessness, and worthlessness over a long period of time. Those feelings can interfere with normal daily activities. Volunteers are needed to help care for people with varying degrees of mental illness.

When you look at the options, you'll be sure to find something that fits you. Volunteering for individuals can be rewarding emotionally.

Many volunteers help as a receptionist or with answering the phone.

Points to Consider: PeopleMatters

What's the difference between a chronic disease and an infectious disease?

Describe several ways volunteers help reduce the effects of disease.

There have been over 25,000 AIDS deaths in people ages 20–24. At what age(s) do you suppose many of these people contracted HIV infection? Why do you think so?

How might a teen volunteer to help the hungry and homeless?

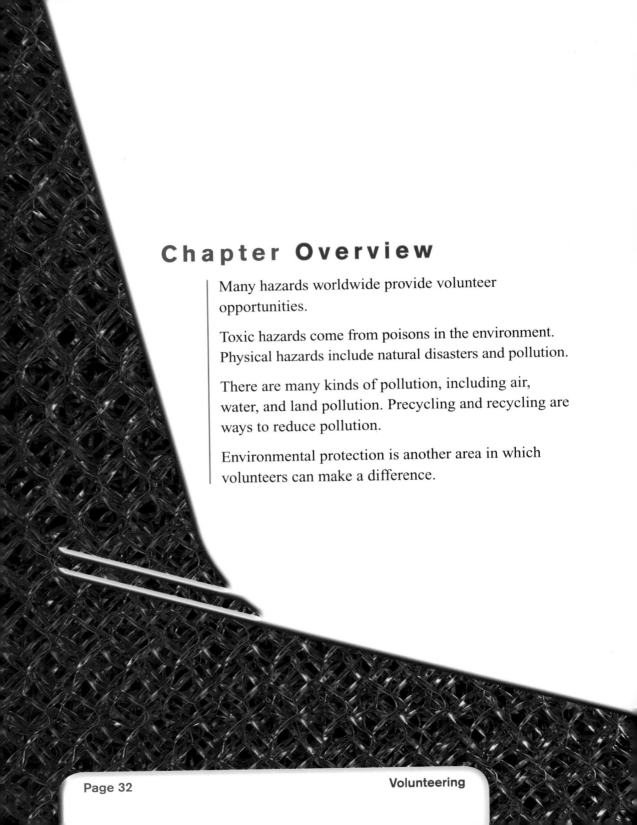

Chapter Overview

Many hazards worldwide provide volunteer opportunities.

Toxic hazards come from poisons in the environment. Physical hazards include natural disasters and pollution.

There are many kinds of pollution, including air, water, and land pollution. Precycling and recycling are ways to reduce pollution.

Environmental protection is another area in which volunteers can make a difference.

CHAPTER 4

Volunteering for the Community and Environment

People's health depends on many factors, such as the environment. This includes plants and animals, water, air, and soil. The quality of the environment can tremendously influence people's health.

Chemical hazards, pollution, and natural disasters threaten people around the world. These **ExternalMatters** provide opportunities to volunteer. Educating yourself and participating in cleanup campaigns are ways that you can serve. Environmental volunteers often focus on a particular environmental issue. Maybe you'll want to get involved with some of these areas.

Toxic chemicals may pose a threat to human health.

Toxic Chemical Hazards

Changes in society and technology continually bring new substances into the environment. Today, roughly 65,000 manufactured chemicals are used throughout the world. The health risks of many of these chemicals are not fully understood. These substances can cause harm throughout a person's life.

Some substances even can harm a developing baby inside its mother. These substances are called teratogens (from the Greek word *teras,* meaning "monster"). Teratogens include lead, mercury, radiation, and pathogens, or disease-causing organisms. Even common medicines such as aspirin and antibiotics have potential danger to the unborn. Antibiotics are prescription drugs that fight infections that pathogens cause. Exposure to certain environmental substances even can cause cancer in unborn children.

Toxic chemicals are substances poisonous to living organisms and include lead, mercury, and pesticides. Many toxic hazards occur in the environment. For example, arsenic occurs in small amounts in some foods, tobacco, wood preservatives, and pesticides. It can be extremely dangerous to people who regularly come in contact with it. Asbestos is a mineral commonly found in the insulation of older homes, schools, and buildings. Serious lung diseases can result when someone inhales asbestos fibers.

Natural disasters such as tornadoes can cause great damage.

Physical Hazards

Physical hazards are another area of environmental concern. These include natural disasters such as floods or earthquakes, and pollution. You can find many opportunities to help people in need.

Natural Disasters

Natural disasters often strike with little warning. Advances in weather technology have increased the warning time for the people in a community. This allows them time to get to safety and protect themselves. Yet, natural disasters can devastate a community's people and property.

Hurricanes, floods, earthquakes, tornadoes, and blizzards are just some natural disasters. They can cause major problems. The CDC estimates that natural disasters in the United States have killed 3 million people during the past 20 years. They have harmed an additional 800 million people.

Volunteers can help reduce the potential harmful effects of storms. Volunteers can help build water and wind barriers. They can clean up, serve food, or protect property. They might donate services, help with child care, or gather supplies. People who experience a natural disaster welcome and sincerely appreciate volunteers.

FAST FACT

The earthquake with the largest loss of life occurred January 24, 1556, in Shaanxi, China. It killed 830,000 people. In 1989, an earthquake rocked the San Francisco Bay area, killing 62 people.

Robbyn, Age 16

Robbyn had heard about the terrible floods in a city not far from where she lived. The news reported that buses were available to bring volunteers to the area to help with cleanup. Robbyn and her father decided to help. They took a bus to the area. They were able to help move out and throw away furniture that floodwaters had damaged. The people she was helping were glad just to have a hand with this unpleasant work. After three days, Robbyn was tired but glad she had taken the time to help.

To help with natural disasters worldwide, contact a representative from UNICEF—United Nations Children's Fund. (This was formerly United Nations International Children's Emergency Fund.) If you want to be involved at the local level, contact your nearest American Red Cross organization. It's listed in the phone book.

Volunteering

Another kind of pollution is noise pollution. Sound is measured in decibels. A whisper is 30 decibels. A lawnmower is 90 decibels and may damage your hearing after you're exposed to it for eight hours. A rock concert is 120 decibels and may damage your hearing after seven minutes. A jet taking off is 140 decibels and may damage your hearing immediately.

Pollution

Pollution is contamination of the environment. People and their activities cause most pollution. Common types of pollution include air, water, and land pollution. Volunteers can help reduce these threats to environmental health.

Air pollution. People have known for centuries that the air can make them sick. Our air is about 20 percent oxygen and 80 percent nitrogen. Unfortunately, air can become polluted from car exhaust, factories, and homes.

Carbon monoxide is a poisonous gas from the incomplete burning of fuels, wood, and tobacco. It contributes to pollution. So do motor vehicles with inefficient engines and faulty exhaust systems.

Volunteers might be able to organize carpools to reduce auto use. They also might start a campaign for people to use bikes or buses or to walk instead of using their cars.

Precycling and recycling. Precycling means eliminating waste before it's created. For example, you may be able to buy fast food in Styrofoam boxes or fast food with little packaging. The choice of less packaging creates less waste to start with.

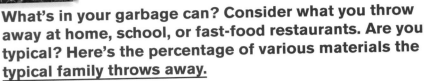

What's in your garbage can? Consider what you throw away at home, school, or fast-food restaurants. Are you typical? Here's the percentage of various materials the typical family throws away.

Paper/paperboard: 38 percent (U.S.), 33 percent (Canada)

Food and yard trimmings: 25 percent (U.S.), 33 percent (Canada)

Metals and plastics: 16 percent (U.S.), 20 percent (Canada)

Glass: 7 percent (U.S.)

Wood: 6 percent (U.S.)

Recycling refers to collecting and reusing many forms of waste. This includes newspaper, plastics, aluminum cans, and glass bottles. Americans currently recycle about 27 percent of their solid waste.

Precycling and recycling can reduce community landfill problems. They also save money, natural resources, and energy. You and others can do your share to reduce the amount of waste in your community.

Buy products with minimal packaging.

Reuse products.

Learn what items can be recycled.

Establish recycling bins in your home and school.

Encourage people and businesses to sell products in recyclable material and to recycle.

Protecting water and wildlife. Lakes and rivers usually are noticeable, beneficial parts of a community. They provide beautiful scenery, recreation, and a habitat for birds, fish, and animals. However, especially in populated areas, they need care, attention, and protection. Volunteers can provide that. Call a local forest preserve, zoo, or park office for information on opportunities.

Volunteers can educate the community in ways to keep the waters healthy. This may include not dumping materials such as oil or paint down street drains. These often run directly into lakes and rivers. Volunteers can remind boaters to check and clean boats and motors. Volunteers can watch for substances that shouldn't travel from lake to lake, such as water plants that invade and destroy lake habitats. Other volunteers may work to control chemical runoff.

There are endless possibilities of ways to volunteer to protect the environment. By working on local problems, volunteers improve the quality of life for everyone who lives in a community.

Points to Consider: ExternalMatters

Give three examples of toxic chemical hazards. What are some suggestions to reduce these hazards?

Give three examples of natural disasters. Which are most likely to occur where you live?

List organizations in your community where you could volunteer.

What are the major contributors to air pollution? What are some suggestions to reduce air pollution?

Chapter Overview

Donations are an important part of volunteering.

Blood transfusions are transfers of blood from person to person.

There are four blood types: A, B, AB, and O. A quiz can help you see what you know about donating blood.

You can donate your body organs. Such donations can save a life or advance medical research.

CHAPTER 5

Volunteering by Donation

Using time, skill, energy, and money are common ways that people give of themselves. However, some volunteers really do give part of themselves. This chapter deals with **DonationMatters**, which could save a life. This might include giving blood. It might mean giving your kidneys, heart, eyes, or other organs to be used in the future.

Blood Transfusions

Most people are sick or injured at some time. Usually, it's not life threatening. However, some people do have life-threatening conditions requiring blood transfusions, such as being injured in a car crash. This transfer of blood from one person to another occurs to replace a large loss of blood. A transfusion using a person's own blood is possible if the blood has been donated ahead of time. If blood lost in surgery is collected and cleansed, it can be used in this way, too.

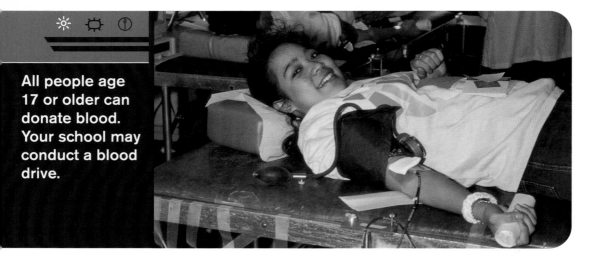

All people age 17 or older can donate blood. Your school may conduct a blood drive.

One example of a life-threatening need for a transfusion is leukemia. This disease includes several cancers of blood-forming tissues such as bone marrow. An abnormal increase of disease-fighting white blood cells characterizes leukemia. The cause of leukemia is unknown, but genes, certain viruses, and exposure to radiation may play a role.

The use of anticancer drugs and medications is called chemotherapy. It's effective against some forms of leukemia, especially those occurring in children. Bone marrow transplants are also often effective. This intensive chemotherapy and radiation treatment destroys harmful tissue and the bone marrow. An injection of disease-free marrow cells then restores the marrow.

As people grow older, the chances increase that they'll experience serious or life-threatening conditions requiring blood transfusions. These conditions frequently are related to problems such as heart disease, cancer, or injuries.

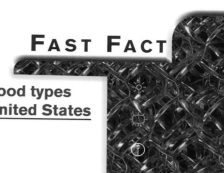

Percentage of blood types (groups) in the United States

Type	Percentage
O:	45 percent
A:	41 percent
B:	10 percent
AB:	4 percent

Blood Types

Blood is divided into four types, or groups: A, B, AB, and O. Your blood type is inherited and is determined by whether you have certain substances in your blood.

People with blood type O are universal donors. They can give blood to all other groups. People with blood type AB are universal recipients. They can accept blood from all other groups.

In whole blood transfusions, the donor's blood group must fit with the recipient's. If not, the red blood cells will burst and clump. This can result in kidney damage and death. When whole blood is not needed or unavailable, the fluid part of the blood, or plasma, may be transfused.

The need for donated blood is great. Each year, blood donations have decreased by about 1 percent. However, blood need is increasing about 1 percent per year. Nearly 95 percent of us will require a blood transfusion at some point.

What do you know about donating blood? Take this quick quiz to find out.

What About Donating Blood?

Read items 1–7 below. On a separate sheet of paper, write your answer to each question.

1. How old do you have to be to donate blood?
   a) 14   b) 17   c) 21

2. When are you too old to be a blood donor?
   a) 55   b) 65   c) never

3. How often can you give blood?
   a) Every 30 days   b) Every 56 days   c) Every 90 days

4. When donating blood, are you safe from contracting infectious blood diseases such as HIV or hepatitis B?
   a) Yes   b) No

5. How much should a blood donor weigh?
   a) 70 pounds (31.5 kilograms)
   b) 90 pounds (40.5 kilograms)
   c) 110 pounds (49.5 kilograms)

6. How much blood is donated each time?
   a) One pint   b) One quart   c) One gallon

7. How long does the entire blood donation process take?
   a) About 1 hour   b) About 2 hours   c) About 3 hours

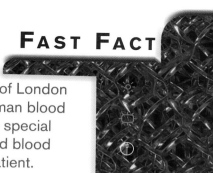

In 1818, surgeon James Blundell of London performed the first successful human blood transfusion. Blundell invented two special pieces of equipment that permitted blood to be transferred from donor to patient.

Answers

1. b) You must be at least 17 years old to donate blood in the United States.

2. c) You're never too old to donate blood.

3. b) You may donate blood every 56 days, or six times per year. It takes about two months to replace all of your red blood cells.

4. a) Yes, you're safe. Materials used to collect blood are used once and then thrown away. This makes the spread of infection through donation impossible.

5. c) A blood donor must weigh at least 110 pounds (49.5 kilograms).

6. a) One pint. It takes about 10 minutes to fill the pint-size bag.

7. a) The entire process takes about 1 hour.

In the United States each year, approximately 20,000 lives are saved through organ donation and transplantation.

You may not yet be 17 years old. This means you can't donate blood yet. However, you can still volunteer your services and contribute to the blood donation effort. Volunteers can perform many tasks. They can recruit people, register donors, assist medical staff, answer phones, or help raise funds.

Volunteer to Be an Organ Donor

Every year, family members, friends, and strangers who act in an emergency save the life of hundreds of people. Perhaps the rescuer knew CPR, rescue breathing, or other first aid. Most of us, though, will never have the opportunity to save a human life. That role usually belongs to medical staff, police, and firefighters.

There is one way you can save a human life. This is through organ donation. Your organs can make a tremendous difference to a patient and the patient's family. Your organs could contribute to research that seeks cures for diseases or conditions such as cancer or diabetes.

Ed was excited finally to get his driver's license! It had taken hard work and lots of practice, but he had passed the driver's exam. As he filled out his first license application, he saw a sentence about becoming an organ donor. He knew that his mom and stepfather both were donors. He had told them he wanted to be a donor, too. Ed decided it was an easy way to help someone else. All he had to do was check the box that said, "Do you wish to become an organ donor?"

Organ donation often sounds frightening, but it doesn't have to be. There are cases where people can donate without dying. For example, you may donate one of your two kidneys to someone who needs one. You may donate bone marrow to someone with cancer. You may donate part of your liver.

However, usually you don't donate body parts until after death. Death occurs when the brain, brain stem, and heart stop functioning. The brain needs oxygen and other nutrients to survive. When brain cells don't receive enough oxygen and nutrients, the brain dies. This is sometimes true of head injuries. Once brain cells die, they aren't replaced.

Death from a heart attack, or cardiac death, is different from brain death. Cardiac death is when the heart and lungs suddenly stop functioning. People who die in this manner can't donate their organs. When the heart stops, then blood doesn't circulate. When blood doesn't circulate, the organs receive no oxygen and are damaged. People who die of a heart attack, however, still may donate the eyes or other body tissues.

Tell your family about your decision to become or not become an organ donor. That way, they can be sure to carry out your wishes about donating organs.

Look at the following self-assessment. Can you answer these questions about organ donation?

What About Organ Donation?

On a separate sheet of paper, write whether you think the following six statements are true or false.

1. Brain death is the same as a coma.

2. Human organs can be sold in the United States.

3. Donated organs can be used for research.

4. The heart and lungs can be preserved for transplantation for about six hours after their removal.

5. The donor's family pays for donated organs.

6. The person getting the transplant knows the organ donor.

Answers

1. **False:** A person in a coma continues to have brain activity and therefore hasn't died.

2. **False:** According to the Uniform Anatomical Gift Act of 1968, human organs can't be bought or sold.

3. **True:** If an organ can't be used for transplantation, it may be useful for research.

4. **True:** Different organs can be preserved for varying amounts of time. The heart and lungs are good for about six hours. The liver and intestines are good for about 24 hours. The kidney is good for about 48 hours.

5. **False:** There's no charge to the donor's family.

6. **Usually false:** Generally the identities of both the recipient and the donor remain confidential. Rarely, a meeting can be scheduled between a donor's family and the person who received the organ.

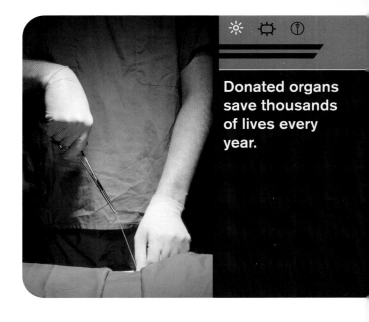

Donated organs save thousands of lives every year.

If you're seriously injured, you may wonder if the doctors are trying hard to help you. Don't worry. The medical staff trying to save your life aren't the same people associated with organ donation.

Points to Consider: DonationMatters

What determines which blood types can be transfused to another person?

How do you feel about giving blood? Explain.

What organs can be donated? Which one can be preserved for the longest period of time?

Why do you think some people fear donating blood and organs?

Chapter Overview

No matter what your interests are, you can find a volunteer opportunity in that area.

By volunteering, you can get experience in areas you might want to consider as a career. Volunteer activities look good on a resumé.

Virtual volunteering is another way to serve. People with all types of physical disabilities can volunteer in this way.

There are 10 pieces of advice to follow as you get started with volunteering.

CHAPTER 6

☼

Practical Volunteering

Being a volunteer is a commitment you make. Make volunteering work for you. **VolunteeringMatters** actually can bring you together with family and friends. It also may be a step toward exploring what you'll choose for a career.

Getting Involved

Do you like sports? In most communities, parks and other organizations offer sports programs for kids. These programs usually depend on volunteers to lead activities. Coaches are needed for soccer, basketball, hockey, baseball, and football. Coaches also are needed for activities such as karate, dancing, and volleyball.

Do you like nature? Many nature centers need volunteers to assist with their nature education programs for kids. Volunteers help kids better understand aspects of nature, from fall leaves turning color to the animals around them.

Do you like kids? The health and well-being of children is very important to communities. Unfortunately, many children don't receive the nurturing that's so vital for positive growth and development. As a volunteer, you can positively influence a young person. Volunteer to read to kids at a shelter. Join an organization like Big Brothers or Big Sisters.

Child mentoring programs are also key parts of many communities. Mentors are people who may meet with a child periodically to assist with homework or just to be a friend. Some communities have "e-mentors" for people who can't get together personally. They may be able to chat by way of e-mail.

Child advocates help kids who have been abused or neglected. Sadly, thousands of young children have been taken from their parents for safety reasons. Many of these kids need someone to talk with and count on to be there for them.

Young people aren't the only group needing volunteers. The older members of communities could use your time and energy. You can help out at senior care centers and nursing homes. You can answer telephones, serve meals, help with games and films, or assist in art and music projects. Often, just a visit is the highlight of a resident's day.

Older people who still live at home often appreciate help in their daily activities. They may need lawn care, grocery shopping, shoveling, or help with the mail.

As a member of a youth organization, you may be part of group volunteer projects.

Lester, Age 14

"I sell magazines for a food shelf. I also pick up garbage in my neighborhood. My brother, next-door neighbor, and Gramps all help me do that. I think volunteering for something makes you a better person. If more people volunteered, it would really bring the people of the Earth together like friends."

Ways to Get Involved

Join a youth organization that includes service to others in its mission. As a member, you'll get to participate in group volunteer projects with the other teens in your organization. This gives you a circle of friends as well as service opportunities. Look into youth groups at the YMCA or YWCA, your place of worship, or Girl or Boy Scouts.

Does your school have a club or extracurricular group that does volunteer service? You may be required to do community service before you graduate. If so, a volunteer coordinator's office or school counselor can suggest nearby agencies that accept student help.

You're probably under 18 years old. It's true that some organizations require volunteers to be at least 18 years old. However, there are numerous opportunities for younger volunteers. The good news is that you can get to do some things that you would never get hired to do.

If you like animals, consider volunteering at an animal shelter.

Volunteering in a Potential Career

Have you thought about a future career? As a teen, you're probably thinking about all sorts of possibilities. You've also probably eliminated some choices. The great thing about volunteering is you can get exposure to all sorts of jobs—even your dream jobs.

Do you like medicine? Most hospitals have plenty of volunteer possibilities. No, you won't get to do heart surgery, deliver a baby, or take X rays. But you can get in on lots of the hospital action. And because of your help, the hospital patients may receive enriched care that results in faster and better recovery. You may be asked to hold babies in the nursery or spend time with young patients. You might work in the health education center or even make baby blankets.

Do you like animals? Consider working at a veterinarian's office, animal shelter, humane society, or zoo. You may be asked to greet and guide visitors, help exhibit animals, or work at special events.

Do you like people? Many volunteer jobs exist in airports, in retail stores, in legal settings, on the ski slopes, or at community theaters.

Everyone's dreams are different. But there's a good chance that a volunteer opportunity exists that matches your dream. Take a risk, follow your dream. Explore the opportunities!

Maria wants to become a carpenter. She knew that her experiences with Habitat for Humanity would look good when she applied for a job. For three years, Maria helped build homes, learning about plumbing, electricity, roofing, and how a house works. She was already a pretty good carpenter. Of course, she was glad to help families to afford and live in their own home. And she planned to continue to volunteer for many years to come. However, Maria had a head start on other people who might want the same job she did. It was the perfect arrangement.

Think "Resumé"

Have you ever looked back at your school years and wondered how the time passed so quickly? In the not-so-distant future, you may need to think about applications for jobs or future schools. A resumé is a record highlighting your personal experiences and skills. Often, a strong resumé will help you stand out from others making the same application. Many employers and schools are interested in people involved in their school and community. Be sure to put your volunteer work on your resumé!

Remember to list your abilities such as school attendance record, grades, hobbies, and interests. Do you know how to use a computer? Do you have good math or communication skills? Do you speak a foreign language? Are you involved in school programs or activities? Are you accurate with details? Are you friendly? Are you willing try a new experience?

Volunteering online is a way people with a disability can volunteer.

Virtual Volunteering

Some teens want to volunteer for certain issues but can't because of time or distance problems. They may have home, family, or school commitments, or a disability. Using the Internet is one way around these challenges. This type of volunteering is often referred to as virtual volunteering. It means that volunteer tasks are completed partly or completely via the Internet. It's also called online volunteering, cyber service, telementoring, and teletutoring.

Virtual volunteering programs allow greater participation of people who might find volunteering difficult or impossible. This, in turn, allows organizations to benefit from the additional talent and resources of more volunteers. People with disabilities volunteer for the same reasons as anyone else. They want to contribute their time and energy to improving the quality of life. They want challenging, rewarding, educational service projects that address needs of a community. They want projects that provide them with outlets for their enthusiasm and talents.

Before you jump into virtual volunteering, take this quick readiness check.

Should I Volunteer Online?

Read items 1–10 below. On a separate sheet of paper, answer yes or no for each item. These items are about traits virtual volunteers need.

1. Do you have regular access to the Internet?	Yes	No
2. Do you have good writing and communication skills?	Yes	No
3. Do you stick to deadlines?	Yes	No
4. Can you work well without direct supervision?	Yes	No
5. Are you self-motivated?	Yes	No
6. Can you pace yourself well?	Yes	No
7. Can you avoid overcommitting to other activities?	Yes	No
8. Can you set a time of day when you'll work?	Yes	No
9. Will your work area be free of distractions?	Yes	No
10. Is this the right time for you?	Yes	No

If you answered no to any of the above questions or had difficulty answering some of them, perhaps you're not ready for virtual volunteering.

Good Advice

The Hiroshima Volunteer Network in Japan offers this advice about volunteering. As you see, good advice is worldwide!

1. Do what you can. Start with something easy and gradually move to something more challenging.

2. Don't be too ambitious. An easier but continued activity will win people's trust and help you to stay involved. Say no if you think something is too hard.

3. Think of the other person. Any volunteer activity involves people who need help and people who give it. The wishes of people you're trying to help should come before your wants.

4. Keep your promises. This is true even if they're casual promises. Keep your word about things such as when you'll visit and what you'll do. Keep your promises to children, too.

5. Be aware of your limits. You can do only so many volunteer activities. There's also a limit to the amount of time you can spend.

6. Don't sacrifice your family, schoolwork, activities, or job for your volunteer activities. Often, volunteers spend less time at home. This may cause friction within families. Obtaining the understanding of the people closest to you is important.

7. Keep secrets. In the course of your activities, you may learn information about other people. Never pass this information on to others. It will help you create trust.

8. Keep personal beliefs out. Volunteer activities are about respecting other people's rights. Trying to make them believe the same things you do disrespects their rights. Keep your beliefs to yourself while using them to help others.

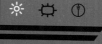

Anyone can be a volunteer. But it's not going to happen if you don't get up and do it.

9. Don't take money or goods. To maintain your independence, don't accept money or other kinds of compensation. Giving of your time, effort, and emotional support is the best way to help others.

10. Learn from your work. Volunteer activities provide a wonderful opportunity for personal development and self-fulfillment. Volunteering helps you learn from those whom you're trying to help.

Go for It

You might want to volunteer. You're not going to do it only by reading this book. You have to make it happen. Go out and make a difference!

Points to Consider: VolunteeringMatters

In what ways can volunteering help you with a potential career?

What is virtual volunteering? What are some of its advantages and disadvantages?

What advice would you give teens considering a volunteer position?

NOTE

At publication, all resources listed here were accurate and appropriate to the topics covered in this book. Addresses and phone numbers may change. When visiting Internet sites and links, use good judgment. Remember, never give personal information over the Internet.

Internet Sites

Make a Difference Day
www.usaweekend.com/diffday/index.html
Project ideas and guides for volunteer activities, plus many links to other volunteer organizations

Pitch In
www.pitchin.org/edition1/table.html
Articles on volunteering, written by teens

ServeNet
www.servenet.org
Links to information about volunteering, including virtual volunteering

Youth Cyberstation
www.pch.gc.ca/Cyberstation/html/home_e.htm
Information and links on volunteering in Canada, what it means, and how to do it

Youth Service America
www.ysa.org
Resource center of over 200 organizations committed to increasing the opportunities for young Americans to serve

For More Information

Useful Addresses

American Red Cross
Attention: Public Inquiry Office
431 18th Street Northwest
Washington, DC 20006
www.redcross.org
Provides relief to disaster victims, blood to hospital patients, and safety training to the public

Canadian Lung Association
3 Raymond Street, Suite 300
Ottawa, ON K1R 1A3
CANADA
www.lung.ca
Information on healthy breathing

FamilyCares
PO Box 1083
New Canaan, CT 06840
www.familycares.org
Opportunities for people to help others in their local and global communities

Impact Online
325 "B" Forest Avenue
Palo Alto, CA 94301
www.impactonline.org
Advice for potential volunteers, plus virtual volunteering opportunities

For Further Reading

Duper, Linda Leeb. *160 Ways to Help the World: Community Service Projects for Young People.* New York: Checkmark, 1996.

Erlbach, Arlene. *The Kids' Volunteering Book.* Minneapolis: Lerner, 1998.

Fairview Press. *How We Made the World a Better Place: Kids and Teens Write on How They Changed Their Corner of the World.* Minneapolis: Fairview, 1998.

Lewis, Barbara A., and Pamela Espeland. *The Kid's Guide to Social Action: How to Solve the Social Problems You Choose and Turn Creative Thinking Into Positive Action.* Minneapolis: Free Spirit, 1998.

Perry, Susan K. *Catch the Spirit: Teen Volunteers Tell How They Made a Difference.* New York: Franklin Watts, 2000.

Glossary

antibiotic (an-ti-bye-OT-ik)—prescription drug that fights infections that pathogens cause

cardiopulmonary resuscitation (CPR) (car-dee-oh-PUHL-muh-ner-ee ri-suhss-uh-TAY-shuhn)—technique to revive a person whose heart has stopped

consent form (kuhn-SENT FORM)—a written agreement that identifies a volunteer's role in an organization

developing world (di-VEL-uh-ping WURLD)—countries where housing, food, education, health care, and other services may be poor or are just beginning

donation (doh-NAY-shuhn)—a gift of time, talent, effort, money, or such things as blood, kidneys, or eyes; someone who donates expects nothing in return.

epidemic (ep-uh-DEM-ik)—a widespread outbreak of disease

pathogen (PATH-uh-jen)—a disease-causing organism

resumé (REZ-uh-may)—a brief written description of education, skills, volunteer efforts, goals, and names of adults who can be contacted on your behalf

teratogen (tuh-RAT-uh-juhn)—a harmful substance such as lead, mercury, or pathogens

transfusion (transs-FYOO-zhuhn)—transfer of blood from one person to another

universal donor (yoo-nuh-VUR-suhl DOH-nuhr)—someone who can give blood to all other groups; people with blood type O are universal donors.

universal recipient (yoo-nuh-VUR-suhl ri-SIP-ee-uhnt)—someone who can accept blood from all other groups; people with blood type AB are universal recipients.

virtual volunteering (VUR-choo-wuhl vol-uhn-TIHR-ing)—the use of the Internet to identify volunteers or increase ways people might provide service

Index

advice about volunteering, 58–59
AIDS, 24, 25–27
air pollution, 33, 37
American Cancer Society, 23
American Red Cross, 36
animals, 11, 33, 54
antibiotics, 34
application forms, 17
arsenic, 34
asbestos, 34

"Black Death," 25
blizzards, 35
blood
    donation, 7, 41–46
    transfusions, 41–42, 45
    types, 43
Blundell, James, 45
bone marrow, 42, 47

calories, 10
Canadian Lung Association, 23
cancer, 23, 34, 42, 46, 47
carbon monoxide, 37
cardiopulmonary resuscitation (CPR),
    24, 46
careers, 51, 54
Centers for Disease Control and
    Prevention (CDC), 25, 35
chemicals, toxic, 33, 34
chemotherapy, 42
children, 29, 35, 42, 52, 58
clubs, 53
coaching, 51
contacting organizations, 16

death and organ donation, 47, 48, 49
disabilities, 56
diseases, 21, 23–27, 28, 34
donations, 41–49
    blood, 7, 41–46
    eyes, 47
    kidneys, 47
    livers, 47
    organs, 41, 46–49
DonationMatters, 41

earthquakes, 35, 36
education, 29, 39, 51, 56
emotional crisis, 28
environment, 5, 33–39
ExternalMatters, 33

family, 8, 9, 18–19, 24, 27, 38, 46, 47,
    51, 53, 56, 58
fitness, 10
floods, 7, 35
food shelves, 28
friends, 7, 8, 9, 18–19, 27, 28, 46, 51,
    53
fund-raising, 7, 24–27, 46

garbage, 38

hazards, 33, 34–35
health, 23, 33, 34
Hiroshima Volunteer Network, 58
HIV, 24, 25–26
homelessness, 6, 7, 28, 29–30
hospitals, 24, 54
hunger, 28
hurricanes, 35

Index Continued

interests, 5, 10, 11, 15, 16, 17, 19, 55
Internet, 56

Joint United Nations Programme on
    HIV/AIDS, 26

kidney donation, 47
knowledge, 7, 12

lead, 34
leukemia, 42
liver donation, 47

Make a Difference Day, 9
medical issues, 5. *See also* diseases;
    health
mental illness, 30
mentors, 52
mercury, 34

natural disasters, 21, 33, 35–36
nature, 51
NextMatters, 15
noise pollution, 37

organ donation, 41, 46–49
    self-assessment, 48
    and death, 47, 49

pathogens, 34
PeopleMatters, 21
pesticides, 34, 39
plasma, 43
pollution, 33, 35, 37–39
precycling, 37–38

radiation
    toxic, 34
    treatment, 42

recycling, 37–38
resumés, 55

self-assessments, 7
    organ donation, 48
    reasons for volunteering, 8–9
    volunteering online, 57
senior citizens, 52
skills, 7, 10, 12, 13, 55
StartingMatters, 5

T-cells, 25
teratogens, 34
time, 10, 11, 18, 57, 58
tornadoes, 35
toxic chemicals, 33, 34
tutoring, 30

United Nations Children's Fund
    (UNICEF), 36

virtual volunteering, 56–57
visiting organizations, 17
volunteer coordinators, 16, 17, 53
volunteering
    advice, 58
    areas, 15, 16, 26, 33
    benefits of, 6, 7
    defined, 6
    online, 56–57
    reasons for, 5, 8–9
VolunteeringMatters, 51

water and wildlife preservation, 39

youth organizations, 53
Youth Service Day, 9

361.3   Wandberg, Robert

WAN   Volunteering

6/03	DATE DUE		